A 3-minute forever book

EAT
YOUR
PEAS

for Daughters™

By cheryl and Julia "mom" Karpen
Gently Spoken Communications

There are only
two lasting bequests we can hope
to give our children.
One of these is roots,
the other is wings.

Holding Carter

To _____

With love from _____

At the heart
of this little book
is a promise.

It's a promise
from me to you
and
it goes like this...

If you ever need
someone to talk to
(really talk to),
someone who will listen
(really listen),
to your worries,
your joys,
and your dreams...

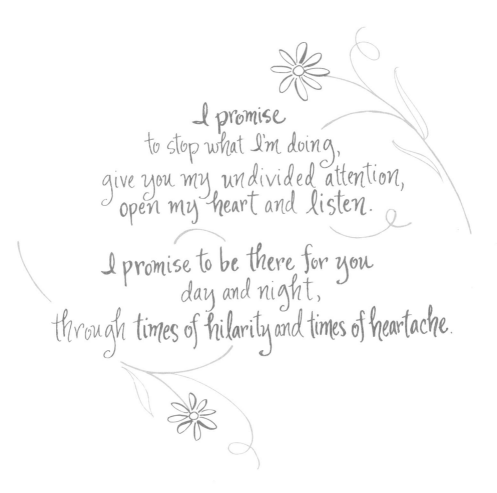

I promise
to stop what I'm doing,
give you my undivided attention,
open my heart and listen.

I promise to be there for you
day and night,
through times of hilarity and times of heartache.

In the meantime,
there are some things
I want to tell you—

like how important you are to me,
how I only want the best for you
and how I wish you joy in life.

Dazzling, irrepressible joy!

I can't wait!

Go ahead and turn the pages.
(Read often for maximum smiles and hugs!)

Here goes...

When you were
first placed in my arms,

I had no idea
what wonders awaited me.

I love you
with all my heart and soul.

Just think...

I was remembering things
about you
before you were able to remember
things for yourself.

Anything you'd like to know?

FIRST WORDS ♡ FIRST DAY OF SCHOOL ♡ FIRST SMILE ♡ FIRST BIRTHDAY ♡ FIRST DRAWING ♡ FIRST TRIP ♡ FIRST LOVE ♡ FIRST FOODS ♡ FIRST STEPS ♡

Beauty comes wrapped in many packages:

a smile,

an intelligent
mind,

an act of kindness,

a loving heart.

You are so beautiful.

May I always know when
to give you room to wander
and wings to fly.

Life is filled with
choices.

Choose carefully.

Always reach for, wait for, work for,
what will make you
feel alive and complete in life.

Keep a **dream** in your pocket
and **faith** in your heart.

Anything is possible!

There is no challenge in life
so big we can't
handle it together.

I'll
always
be there
for
you.

Even in the deepest heartache,
there is grace in
humor.

May we always know how
to make each other **smile**
and give each other
reasons to **hope.**

I can't help but **smile** every time

I think of the person you've become.

I count you among my blessings every day.

Sometimes life
doesn't go as planned
and
not getting what we want
becomes a blessing
in disguise.

There is a plan for you.
Have **faith**.

Be patient and most of all...
Believe.

For good health and a strong spirit, repeat 10 times daily!

I am lovable.

I am loving.

I am loved.

I will always
believe
in you.

There will be times in our life
when **we** simply will not agree
or understand one another.

And that's okay.
One day we may even laugh about it.

Remember when you first learned
our address?

Never forget that
home
is the permanent address of the heart.

Dance wherever you can.
Sing boldly.
Embrace your spirit.
Be your authentic self.
Listen. Forgive. Laugh a lot.
Cultivate lasting friendships.
Live compassionately.
And by all means... have fun!

Live the life
you dream of...
(Go for it!)

Embrace
your gifts...
(You have so very many!)

Be kind
to yourself...
(You are worth it!)

And most of all, stay healthy...

Remember to always...

Eat your peas!

With gratitude...

To my mother, Julia Karpen

I have invited my mother to co-author Eat You Peas for Daughters.
Not only is she a wonderful mother to three grateful daughters,
this woman also happens to be one of the most
remarkable individuals I have ever known.

I am not the only one who thinks so. My sisters and I are honored
to have shared our Mom with other adopted daughters over the
years — girls and women whose own mothers
have passed on or live too far away for a hug.

I like to think of us as Julia's garden...living proof this
amazing woman makes things grow wherever she goes. Planting hope.
Pruning doubt. Cultivating courage and creativity. We are stronger,
straighter...more resilient because of you. Thanks Mom...from all your girls

To Illustrator, Sandy Fougner

You plant LOVE on every page with your spirited artistry.
And it shows.

To Editor, Suzanne Foust

Sometimes I send you weeds and you turn them into beautiful flowers.
Amazing.

♡, Cheryl

About the author

"Eat Your Peas"

In addition to her "passion for PEAS",
Cheryl is the owner of two gift and decorative accessory shops
located in the historic river town of Anoka, Minnesota:
Something Different and Pure Bliss.

An effervescent speaker, Cheryl
brings inspiration, insight and humor to corporations,
church groups and to other professional and community organizations.

Find out more about her at www.SomethingDifferentSisters.com

About the illustrator

Sandy Fougner artfully weaves a love
for design, illustration and interiors with being a
wife and mother of three sons

Eat Your Peas for Daughters™
Copyright 2003, Cheryl Karpen

For more information or to locate a store near you contact:

Gently Spoken Communications
P.O. Box 245
Anoka, Minnesota 55303
1-877-224-7886
www.gentlyspoken.com